CAPTURE CONVERT *Captivate*

How Creatives Can Use Email Marketing To Connect With Their Tribe, Make An Impact, and Create Consistent Income!

LISE CARTWRIGHT

ISBN: 978-0-473-49530-5

For enquiries or bulk copies email lise@hustleandgroove.com

Disclaimer

This book is for informational purposes only.

Some of the information found within the contents of this book is about third party products and services. These Third Party Materials consist of products and opinions expressed by their owners. As such, the author does not assume responsibility or liability for any Third Party material or opinions expressed.

The use of recommended Third Party Material does not guarantee any success and/or earnings related to you or your indie author business. Publication of such Third Part Material is simply a recommendation and an expression of the authors' own opinion of that particular material.

Links to Third Party Resources may be affiliate links, meaning the authors may receive compensation if a service is ultimately purchased from such a link.

YOUR FREE GIFT!

To get the best experience with this book, download the *Capture, Convert, Captivate Workbook* to keep track of all your ideas and next steps for implementation.

You can grab a copy here:
www.hustleandgroove.com/cccworkbook

Table of Contents

Introduction

I couldn't open the email.

What would they have to say? Maybe they're going to tell me how crap my book was… I'm not prepared to hear that from a complete stranger.

Or maybe they are going to say how dumb I am and that I should NOT quit my day job!

What am I meant to do? Everyone is telling me that I need to build my email list now!

But why? That's what I don't understand…

Meet Shy Sue. These are the thoughts she has around using email in her business. She's a writer who loves writing and sharing her message with the world as long as she doesn't have to respond to emails or create landing pages, or any of the other tech stuff.

Shy Sue just wants to write.

Shy Sue has a dream. A big dream. She wants to be the next Oprah Winfrey or Rachael Hollis, impacting millions of women around the world through her words.

Only Shy Sue has no idea how to get her readers to join her email list, nor has she been able to figure out how to create one of those landing page thingees…

Nope. Instead, Shy Sue continues to focus on her writing and hope that one day, a magical publisher will knock on her door and all her dreams will be answered…

Oops. Shy Sue just woke up from her daydream and realizes that if she is going to spread her message and reach millions of readers, it is going to take some action on her part.

But where to start?

Hi! I'm Lise Cartwright, self-confessed shoe fanatic, full-time author of 30+ best selling books and creator of Hustle HQ, a membership site for creative business owners to develop a *Productive Profit Plan* that creates consistent income every month without adding more to-dos to already maxed-out schedules.

Over the past 5 years, I've been honing my craft and connecting with my readers.

Every day, I receive emails from new email subscribers telling me how much they love my energy, my positive vibes, and the knowledge I so willingly share through my books, website and membership site.

But it wasn't always this way.

Oh no. If you met 2014 Lise, you'd be forgiven for thinking you were chatting to the wrong person!

2014 Lise was shy, scared, timid, and not particularly tech-savvy.

'Now Lise', on the other hand, is a chatty, extroverted people-person, always the first to put up her hand to help, and dangerous enough with her good friend Google at her side.

Your version of this might look different, but if you want to connect with your reader, build a tribe of loyal followers, and have raving fans ready to share your message and buy your things, then you have to step out of your comfort zone and approach things a little differently.

WHO THIS BOOK IS FOR

This book is for you. The creative business owner looking to make a real impact in the world.

It's for the writer who longs to hear her message being spread around the world.

It's for the freelancer looking to transition into delivering coaching or digital products.

It's for you if you have a desire to change the world, leave a positive mark, and feel good about the work you do every. single. day.

WHO THIS BOOK IS *NOT* FOR

My friend, if you're reading this and you already have a successful creative business with an audience who loves EVERYTHING you do, then you're not likely to learn much from these pages.

Sure, you'll get a kick out of imagining what my NZ accent really sounds like as you flick through these pages, but that's about it.

So rather than waste your time, go ahead and stop reading now.

If you've already purchased, then ask your online retailer for a refund or gift it to a friend who needs it. You deserve to use your time on what actually benefits you.

IT'S YOUR TIME TO SHINE

Still with me?

Awesome. I'm excited to dive into the pages of Capture, Convert, Captivate and share with you the simple, easy-to-learn way of connecting with your audience, nurturing them like a newborn baby, and wowing them so they stick around forever like they are your BFF.

I'm excited to get started. Honestly. I'm grinning from ear-to-ear as I write this, bouncing in my chair, waiting for you to dive into the first section.

So don't leave me hanging!

Come join me in *Part 1: Capture*, where we're going to start capturing your awesome audience.

It's your time to shine, impact, and change the lives of your ideal leads/customers/clients!

Part 1:

CAPTURE

"The early bird catches the worm..."

~ English Proverb

In this first part of the book, we're going to look at how to capture the attention of your ideal audience.

What makes them stop in their tracks? What makes YOU stop in your tracks…?

Now, before we go any further, I want to assure you that what I'm about to share with you is neither icky nor 'black hat' in any way.

You should treat your audience with the respect and kindness they deserve.

So under no circumstances are you trying to snare them with some gimmicky gifts that don't serve a purpose for your audience.

We are not one of those infomercials!

So what am I talking about here? I'm talking about figuring out what your audience wants right now and fulfilling that need with a digital free gift.

You might hear this referred to as a lead magnet, freebie, opt-in incentive etc.

They are all the same thing. A free digital product that your audience wants and they are willing to hand over their email address to access.

That's what we are going to dive into first.

Finding the best free gift for your audience.

Because without this piece, no amount of "join my newsletter" is going to be enough to entice them to hand over their email address...

Step 1:

CHOOSE A FREE GIFT

Attracting the right people (leads) into your creative business is about creating the right lead magnet (also called a freebie, free gift, incentive) that provides value to your potential client/customer.

Your lead needs to see your lead magnet and go, "Wow! I have to have this. I can't believe it's free!"

How do you do that?

You figure out what your best lead magnet(s) are and create them!

What the heck are lead magnets Lise?

A lead magnet is an incentive/enticement/free gift that you use to get the right leads onto your email list.

In exchange for providing their email address, they receive your lead magnet aka the free gift they have to have.

Now all going well, and in a perfect, happy-creative-business-owner world, every visitor that lands on your website will grab your lead magnet straight away—happy to hand over their email address...

Unless your lead magnet is the *best lead magnet for that person in this moment* in time, they can end up leaving your site without joining your email list. And that's ok. You don't want everyone to join, you just want your *ideal* leads to sign up.

Which is why I want to highlight that a few things need to align before someone hands over their email address...

#1: Your lead magnet needs to be the thing they need right now. It's a case of meeting them where they are at based on where they land on your website. There's no point someone joining your list and not being able to implement your thing.

#2: Your lead magnet also needs to be something that your potential lead feels they can take action on right away. If it looks like too much effort, they'll skip grabbing it, meaning they'll skip joining your email list. Quick wins are what you want to focus on helping them achieve.

Which leads to the question: ***How can you find your best lead magnet for your ideal audience?***

Let's work out what your best lead magnet is by coming up with different ideas. The goal is to have no more than five lead magnets leading into your products or services (funnels).

Ultimately, you should only have 3-5 funnels in place total.

If you're just starting your creative business, one funnel is plenty and 1-2 lead magnets are more than enough to support that funnel.

Keep it simple.

THE 5-PART FRAMEWORK TO YOUR BEST LEAD MAGNET

#1: Brainstorm

I know this sounds kinda simple, but I've always enjoyed making things simple, and brainstorming is the best way to unlock ideas you hadn't considered.

So to get started, grab a piece of paper or whatever you do to take notes, and set a timer for 15 minutes. I find the timer on my iPhone works best.

Here's what you're going to do:

Write down as many ideas as you can for lead magnets that you feel would be the best fit for your ideal customer/client.

A few things to consider before doing this:

- You should think about high-value ideas, like courses, video training, etc.
- Swipe files, templates and checklists are also great ideas
- Avoid ebooks on their own, they have lost a lot of their value… unless they are an existing published ebook, then it could work

Free-write for 15 minutes until you have at least 20 ideas.

Remember, you're focusing on ideas that would work for YOUR ideal audience but also the types of clients/customers you WANT to work with.

#2: Check out your competition
The next step is to see what your competition is doing.

Find your 5-10 closest competitor's websites and check out what they're providing in the way of lead magnets.

Sign up for their lead magnets and see what their autoresponder sequence looks like too.

Caveat: DO NOT COPY THEIR LEAD MAGNET! Instead, think about how you could make it better, provide more value, add to it etc.

Filter your competition's lead magnets through your own goals and purpose:

- What is your ultimate goal with your business?
- Are you selling services or products?
- Are they direct competition or just in a similar niche? If direct, be careful about what you produce, again NO COPYING!

By now you should have a large list of lead magnet ideas, adding more from this competitor research.

#3: Survey your list
Have you ever asked your potential customers/clients what they actually want or need?

I have to admit, I was pretty scared about sending out a survey to my Hustle & Groove email list—until I did it that is!

It was such an amazing experience. I had a lot of responses and most people were happy to answer a few simple questions.

This has led to me being able to provide even more value via my Hustle & Groove emails and private Facebook Group.

So if you haven't surveyed your list, this is something you should do now.

Don't have an email list? For those of you who are just getting started with your creative business or email list, you might not think that you can do this step.

But you can.

Instead of sending an email, simply share your survey on the social media platform(s) that your ideal potential customer/client is hanging out on.

No excuses! You have to do this step if you want to identify the best lead magnet to attract the right leads into your business. Otherwise, you're going to end up with a ton of leads who aren't the right fit, making your business no fun.

This is what it looks like when the wrong leads end up on your email list...

Argh! Why is no-one buying my services? They downloaded my lead magnet, but none of my subscribers seem at all interested in buying my things.

I get comments like "I love your stuff, but have no money." and "I'm too busy." or "Next paycheck, I'll buy."

I have over 1,000 subscribers but not one of them wants my thing. I just don't get it.

This is what we are looking to avoid.

There are a number of reasons why you can end up in this situation. One of those is not understanding your audience and what they want.

Another is providing them with a product or service that they aren't ready for yet.

This is why it's important to survey your target audience and understand who they are and what they want and need.

Never assume you know best.

So coming back to the survey... The most important question you need to ask inside your survey is this:

"What's the #1 biggest challenge you're facing right now in/with [insert your topic here]?"

The next few questions can be things like:

"What would you like to see more of on the site?" (multi-choice, provide them with options!)

"Where are you in [your topic here]?" (multi-choice, starting out, intermediate or advanced)

Make it easy for people to respond and keep it short! No more than five questions is ideal.

Compile the answers and add any new ones to your growing list.

#4: Rank your ideas

Now that you've got a huge list of potential lead magnets, it's time to narrow things down.

SERVICE-BASED BUSINESSES

If you're providing services or consulting, then you need to think about the lead magnet you offer.

You want your lead magnet to relate to your services and lead them into your email sales funnels that will upsell/down-sell them based on the actions they take.

Educational content works best. What do they need to know/do to be able to work with you?

DIGITAL PRODUCT-BASED BUSINESSES

If you're selling products, your lead magnet should provide part of the solution that your (digital) product provides — so they get a taste of how amazing life could be if they had the whole thing.

You'd also want to feed them into your email sales funnels to upsell/down-sell based on the actions they take too.

Remember, you're looking to provide a lead magnet that is high value. In fact, it should be something that your ideal client/customer would pay for.

Some great examples include:

- A resource library (perfect for both a service or product-based business)
- A video course (3-5 videos is the sweet spot)
- Swipe files (email copy works great here)
- Templates (if you're selling ebook/book formatting services, providing them with a template with instructions is a great idea)
- Cheatsheets (great if you've got some special html code that you use to get your site to do something special)

#5: Identify your top three

Identify the top three ideas and then create all three of these lead magnets.

Why limit yourself to one lead magnet right? But know this — if it feels like a lot to create right now, then just do one first. You can do more later.

In fact, if you want to be a smarty pants about it (who doesn't?!) then you should create lead magnets for the different levels that your audience might be at (achieving the 'meet them where they are at' idea):

1. Beginner, just getting started

2. Started, looking to grow
3. Advanced or nearly there

By doing this, you'd have different funnels that would lead into your products or services that meet those needs.

Then you could upsell/downsell based on the actions they took during the email sequences.

Don't worry about this now though. Get the free gift created then worry about the tech stuff later (we'll cover this later in the book too).

But what about the ideas you have left?

With the list of ideas that you've got left, consider which ones fit within your business model (services vs. products) and your overall strategy for your creative business.

Make a plan to review these ideas against the ones you create and see if you can create another for your best-selling product or service… that way, you're offering more ways for someone to get into your funnels!

Only do this once you've got your first 1,000 leads/subscribers. Remember, you're looking for the right leads. The ones that have the biggest potential to be clients/customers. Keep this in mind as we move through the next step.

STEP 2:

CAPTURING YOUR LEADS

Now that you've created your best lead magnets, we need to capture those leads in some way.

But how? I'm glad you asked.

The solution is to create a page where your new leads can go to give you their email address and, in return, they get your amazing free thing aka your best lead magnet(s).

Now, in order to do that you need to give them a place to "opt-in" and give you their email. This is where your website becomes very important because it creates a way for your website visitors to opt-in to the free gift you're offering.

Don't have a website? Not to worry! I've got you covered. We'll talk about your options in a moment.

Now, it might seem super scary to take this step… allowing a way for people to get on your email list. But it's key to your ongoing success.

You want to work with the right clients or customers, right?

You want to automate your income, yes?! Consistent income starts with attracting and capturing the ideal leads. That's what we're focusing on here.

Then we both agree. You need to master this opt-in process.

If you want to help yourself sell more of your amazing thing, you need to be consistently building your email list full of potential customers and clients.

When you build your list and then treat people on your list with care and respect, they will be excited to hear all about your projects.

I want to cover exactly how you can design, write and set up your opt-ins, but first, let's take a deeper look at the types of opt-ins we're going to cover in this book:

- Opt-in Form
- Opt-in Box
- Landing page

Let's get started.

UNDERSTANDING THE OPT-IN PROCESS

I want to cover what each of these opt-in pieces are right now. Later on in the book, you'll actually learn how to create these either through your email service provider (for those who don't have a website yet) or with some of the tools and plugins I recommend.

#1: Landing Pages

Now, let's talk about landing pages. In basic "marketing" terms, a landing page is a single page that has one specific and defined objective. It's also the glue that brings all things into one place for capturing your leads. Your opt-in form lives on this page.

The cool thing about a landing page is that it gives you a few options.

You can set up a landing page on your own website.

Or you can set up a landing page using your email service provider.

You simply point people to the landing page URL to sign up for your email list and download your lead magnet.

It doesn't matter where the landing page is hosted, as long as it provides a place for your ideal lead to leave their email address, you've won.

Anyone who visits your landing page has to make a choice...

They opt-in to grab your free gift or they leave without providing their details.

The goal is to provide a great hook to entice your potential lead; a great graphic that displays the free gift and a way for them to access it.

The decision should be easy for your ideal lead (and work out in your favor).

Here's a few examples of landing pages I'm currently using:

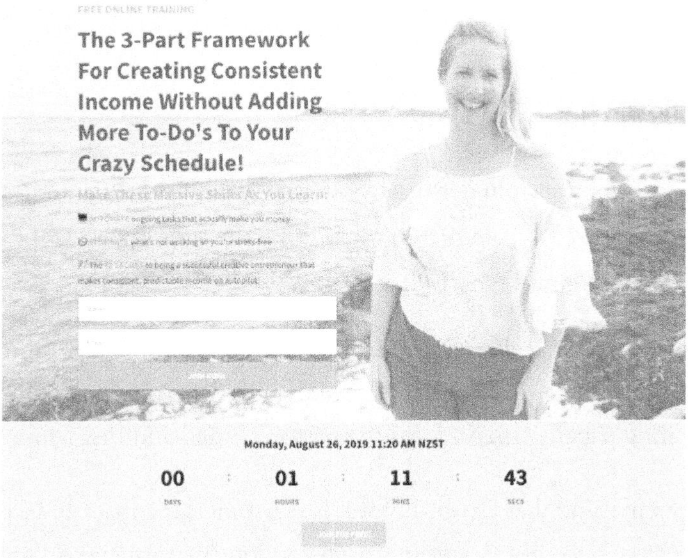

You can see this live at www.hustleandgroove.com/grow.

#2: Opt-in Form
Next, we'll look at what an opt-in form is.

While, on the face of it, opt-in forms and landing pages appear to be similar, there are some important distinctions that I want to point out here.

An opt-in form is often used as a method of collecting email addresses from a website. It's only purpose is to get a visitor to give you their email address. No lead magnet is needed for this to happen.

An opt-in form also makes up part of your landing page. In the previous two examples above, you'll see both opt-in forms on the landing pages... they ask for the person's email and first name.

Keep in mind that an opt-in form is not something that can be put up separately like a landing page. An opt-in form needs to be hosted either on your website (often in the sidebar) or through your email service provider.

You can use your opt-in form to drive sign-ups to your email list. Just like with a landing page, however the results won't be as good.

Now you know the difference between opt-in forms and landing pages. There's one last type of opt-in I want to cover: the opt-in box or subscriber box.

Before we go, let's take a closer look at a few different opt-in forms:

This is the one that was on the second landing page above.

The one below is one that I've used in the sidebar of my blog.

You'll notice the main function is to simply capture details, nothing else.

#3: Opt-In Box

Chances are if you've spent any time browsing some of your favorite websites or blogs, you've come across an opt-in box.

An opt-in box, also called a subscriber box, is a small box on a website that asks for the website visitor to sign up for a mailing list.

These boxes can take all sorts of different forms. They can be a popup, they could be something that slides in at the bottom of a page, or they can be a bar across the top of a website.

There are a number of different plugins you can use to create an opt-in box for your website, or you can also create them through your email service provider (both of which I'll cover a bit more in-depth later on).

An opt-in box is the most simple of the three different types of opt-ins.

While you don't need to put extensive time and effort into designing them, you do need to couple it with your best lead magnets.

Here's what an opt-in box pop-up might look like:

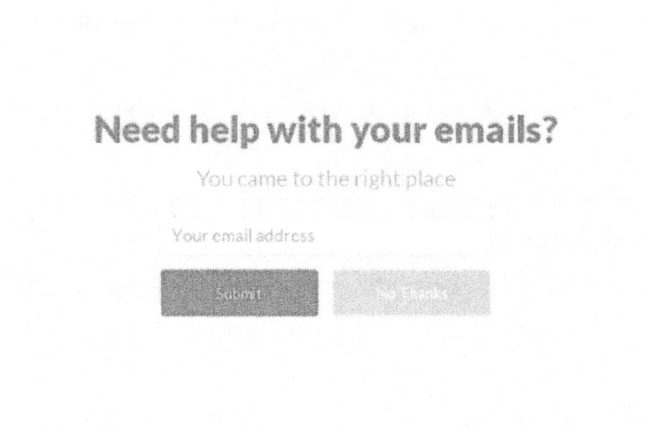

At the end of the day, your goal is to create a landing page to showcase your lead magnet.

CREATE YOUR LANDING PAGE

Let's recap the basics you need to have: a good opt-in form, a landing page, and an opt-in box (if you want to go all-in).

The landing page is a stand-alone page and on it will appear the opt-in form and opt-in box, along with other information to sell yourself and/or your product.

It's very important to remember when it comes to your landing page you don't need to overwhelm visitors with a ton of information.

First, all you want is enough information to get the attention of your ideal lead.

Second, to show the visitor that your lead magnet is amazing and will help them.

Third, to get the visitor to sign up for your email list via your opt-in form.

If you can accomplish all three of these, then you're already way ahead of the game.

If you're just getting started, the next few pages are going to rock.

If you already have an opt-in form and landing page and feel pretty comfortable with what you have, feel free to skip ahead to "deliver your lead magnet".

If you want to take the simple route and use your email service provider for your opt-in forms and landing pages, stick with me here.

Let's get started.

CHOOSING AN EMAIL SERVICE PROVIDER

Now that you know what it takes to create a landing page, you're going to need an email service provider to finish the process.

I recommend email service providers like MailerLite and ConvertKit, and here is where I'll start digging deep into how you can use them and how to set them up.

Why do you need an email service provider you might be wondering...

#1: Professional email capabilities

Well, while you can send out bulk emails to people via your Gmail account now (and you've gotten away with it so far), when you start to try and do that on a larger scale, you need to work with an email service provider or **face getting your Gmail account blacklisted and closed forever!**

Don't have a Gmail account but use something like Outlook or Hotmail? Same deal applies. You needed a dedicated email platform to manage your business leads.

There are a couple of great things that an email service provider is going to do for you.

The most obvious is they will give you a way to collect (and store) your email subscribers. They will also ensure that your emails are delivered… if you choose the right provider, that is.

From there, you will be able to set up your autoresponder series and your regular newsletter.

#2: Easy landing pages

The main thing they will help you achieve are sales funnels that work 24/7 in bringing the right leads into your business and automating your sales.

This starts with your landing page.

But first, let's cover the basics.

There are quite a few email service providers out there.

And I've used a good number of them… from Aweber to MailChimp to ActiveCampaign, MailerLite and ConvertKit.

If you and I were sitting down together having a coffee and cinnamon roll (yum!) and you said to me, "Hey Lise, what's your fav email service provider?" I'd tell you it's ConvertKit.

But ConvertKit isn't free. So if you're budget conscious, then MailerLite or FloDesk are your better options.

But if you want to set yourself up for success right from the start, then ConvertKit is your best option.

Why?

A few reasons:

1. They have amazing deliverability rates, some of the best in the industry. Why does this matter? Because if your emails land in someone's spam or promotions tab, the likelihood of them seeing and opening it are slim.
2. They have beautiful landing pages built-in.
3. You can create visual automations and funnels all in the one screen.

One last thing, the most important thing to consider (beyond your needs) is your personal preference in using a provider.

Don't spend hours agonizing over which one you should pick. Go with the one you like the best.

The good news is, most of these services have a free trial period where you can take them for a test run and see how you like them, including ConvertKit.

Ready to start?

BEGINNER
Get started with simple email service providers.

A couple of the more common ones are MailerLite (www.hustleandgroove.com/mailerlite), ConvertKit (www.hustleandgroove.com/converkitemail), and FloDesk (www.flodesk.com).

Each of these are either free (MailerLite) to start or have a low monthly subscription fee initially so none of them will break the bank to get started.

For most creative business owners who are just getting started, MailerLite is a great option. It's very simple to use and has a clean interface.

You can figure out pretty much everything on your own right away. But, they also have a great set of help documents if you get stuck.

I recommend MailerLite because it offers you quite a bit of flexibility in building your list. You can create your own opt-in forms, which you can then link to your email list and then schedule autoresponders from there.

They also have a number of really nice preset templates you can use for your landing pages, newsletter, and emails.

All you have to do is simply fill in the blanks and you are good to go!

You can learn much more about how to use MailerLite to create opt-in forms and landing pages later on in this chapter.

INTERMEDIATE

For creative business owners who want a little more power and advanced techniques when building their sales funnels, consider options like OptimizePress, Instapage, and LeadPages.

For creative business owners who already have their own website and are more familiar with WordPress, there are also a number of plugins available such as:

- OptinMonster
- OptinForms
- Hellobar
- Sumo

These will give you more than just a vehicle to collect emails. They are actually pretty good "all in one" systems for building a sales funnel.

Here's one created with OptimizePress:

You can use these to create a professional opt-in and landing page in just a few minutes, as well as add in your thank you/download page into the mix. Many, like OptimizePress, are simply drag and drop.

They will do most of the hard work for you on the backend, leaving you to just plug in your bits and pieces.

The good thing about one of these options is you can use them to grow with your business over time, but they aren't too complex to be completely overwhelming from the start.

ADVANCED

For the advanced creative business owner who is looking to build a solid business, automate their income, and is interested in tracking and testing all their traffic... then you want to take a look at some of the more advanced options.

I like using Kajabi or ConvertKit for this. These are going to be a bit more complex and have a learning curve to get started, but the benefit is that they are quite powerful and give you a lot of options.

The main feature of using more advanced tools like Kajabi or ConvertKit is they are an all-in-one process that will take care of building your funnels, opt-ins, and sales processes.

You can build pages that look great and make traveling through your sales funnel easier over the long run.

With a tool like this, you can create a number of landing and opt-in pages. This allows you to offer different incentives for people coming from specific sites and then see which are generating more buzz and converting better.

Here's what a funnel looks like in Kajabi:

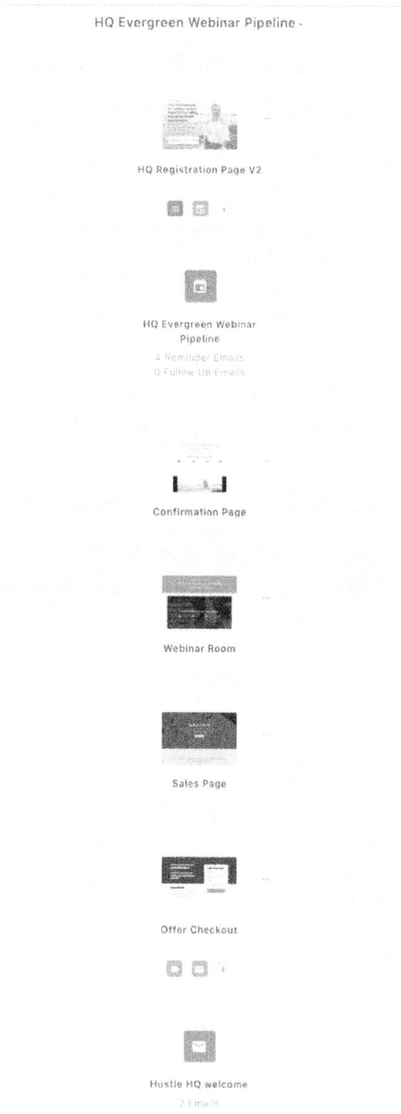

But setting this up is nothing you need to worry about right now.

At this stage of your creative business, all you need to worry about are the most basic functions.

You need an email service provider that will cover the following:

- The ability to collect and store email addresses into a list
- The ability to send out an autoresponder series
- The ability to send out a regular newsletter
- The ability to create landing pages quickly

That's pretty much all you need to start.

Any good email service provider is going to offer you that and a lot more.

Some of the other things you (ideally) want your email service provider to include is the ability to use a plugin that will work with your website to collect the emails, and have a landing page builder built-in.

To start, you don't necessarily need that stuff, but they will be nice to have as you continue to build your list and grow your numbers.

Why MailerLite is Right For You

For beginners or creatives wanting to keep things simple, the email service provider I'd recommend using is *MailerLite*.

There are a couple of reasons why I like MailerLite. One big bonus is that it's free up to 1,000 subscribers.

So for the vast majority of creative business owners who are getting started, MailerLite is a very easy choice.

Once you get over 1,000 subscribers (or send more than 12,000 emails per month), you'll need to upgrade to the next pricing tier, which starts at $10 per month.

MailerLite has well over 30 different templates you can use on your site for opt-ins, or you can make your own if you want.

They offer a WordPress plugin (https://wordpress.org/plugins/official-mailerlite-sign-up-forms/), which allows you to easily capture email subscribers with just a few clicks from within your website.

If you're not using WordPress, you can easily embed the code on any site as well.

Of course, MailerLite also allows you to set up a number of subscriber tags, autoresponders, and subscriber segments as well. So they cover all of your basic needs plus a little more.

GETTING STARTED WITH MAILERLITE

Below I'm going to dive in with some basic tips on getting started. For more detailed information, check out the MailerLite Overview here: https://www.mailerlite.com/video-tutorials/quick-overview.

Once you've signed up for a MailerLite account, the first thing you want to do is create a group (tag).

To do this, follow these steps:

1. Go to the MailerLite dashboard,
2. Go to Subscribers and choose Groups.
3. On the next page, you can fill in the details like the name of your group.

In the example below, you'll see a number of groups already created and the number of subscribers associated with that group.

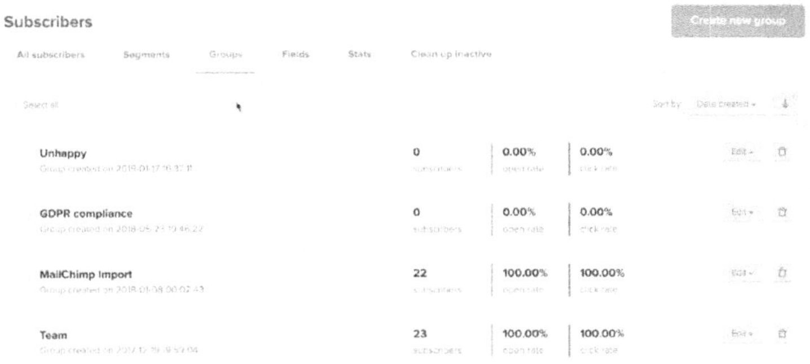

Just a note, if you already have a list of people in a spreadsheet or from another platform, you can easily import, or copy and paste the names into your account.

Remember, only include the emails of people who have specifically given permission (aka have confirmed they have opted in) for you to contact them, no spamming allowed.

Next, create your opt-in form.
Go to your MailerLite dashboard, click on Forms. Make sure that "Landing Pages" is selected.

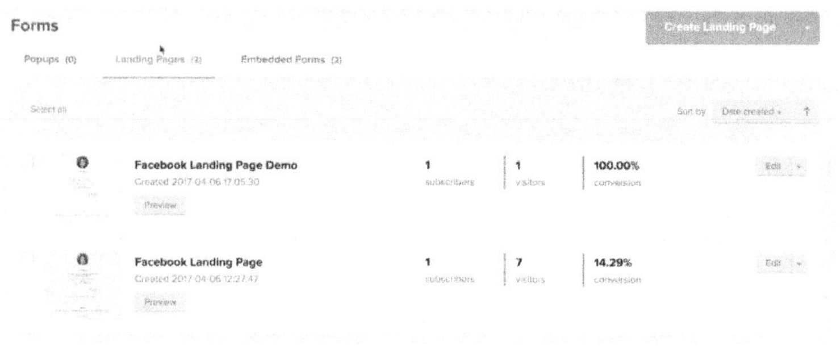

Click "create landing page".

Here you can design your opt-in form/landing page (both are one and the same inside MailerLite. In other ESPs they will be separate.) how you like it. But before you do that, you'll need to give your landing page a name and then choose the group that the landing page is for.

Now you can choose one of MailerLite's templates to get started with.

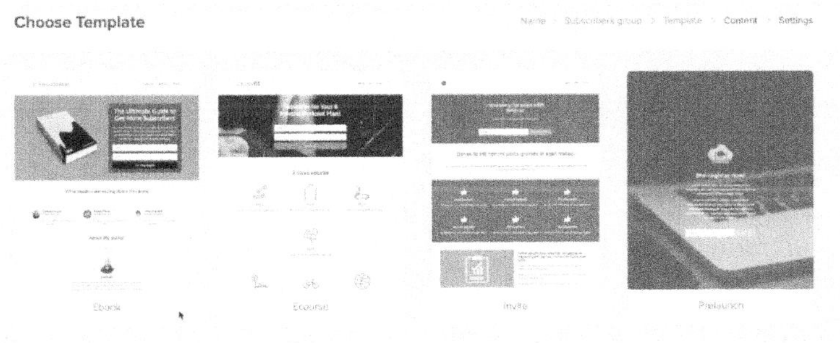

Now you can go ahead and start designing your landing page by updating and changing the presets.

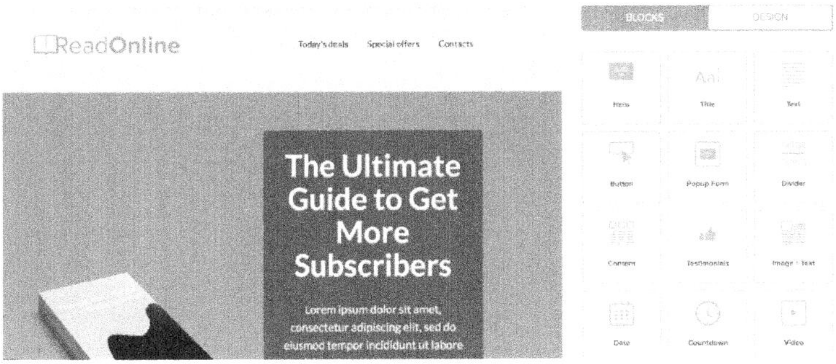

MailerLite has great training videos on every step of this process, so make sure you check them out in their video tutorials knowledgebase here:

https://www.mailerlite.com/video-tutorials.

If you don't have a website you should keep in mind that MailerLite gives the option of giving you an actual link to the opt-in form and landing page that you can also use to promote your lead magnet with.

Once you've got your design set up, click Save and Exit.

Awesome. Now you've created a group and have your opt-in form/landing page set up!

Congratulations. That wasn't so hard now, was it?!

Now, let's focus on getting your lead magnet delivered to your new lead.

In the next section, I'll discuss what that looks like and get you started with your first email to your brand new lead.

STEP 3:

DELIVER YOUR LEAD MAGNET

Now that you've got your lead magnet created and your landing page set up, it's time to make sure that your brand new lead gets what they signed up for.

So how do you deliver your lead magnet?

You have two options:

1. Via email (as a link or direct download)
2. On a specific download page

Those are the only two options.

Pretty simple.

If you want to keep it simple, I'd recommend setting this up to deliver via email, which is very easy to do.

There are a couple of reasons for this.

The first is that you have an opportunity to start connecting with your ideal lead through your initial lead magnet delivery email.

You want them to want to open your emails, so you start "training" them from the beginning to associate your name with an email they want to open.

Most email service providers will give you the option to deliver your lead magnet within the confirmation email. Either as a link or something you upload.

Another option is to use a link from Dropbox or Google Drive, where the lead magnet file is hosted. Some email service providers don't allow you to attach a file, which is why a link is often best.

Now, if you already have a website and want to deliver the free gift via a download page there, that's perfectly fine too.

Here's what that could look like:

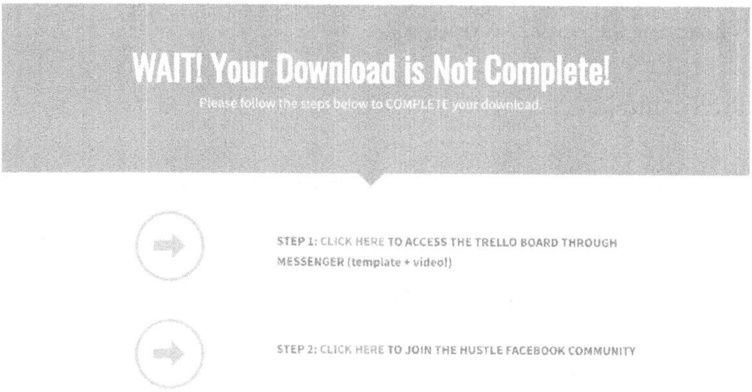

The easy part about using a download page is that many of the tools already have a built-in download/thank you page template that can easily be tied in with your main landing page.

When you're setting up your landing page, simply add a Thank You or Download page to your opt-in page flow.

Then once someone opts into your mailing list, they will be directed to a Download or Thank You page, and on that page, they will be able to access the lead magnet.

Both methods work well for delivery, so the choice is up to you!

Here's an example of what your lead magnet delivery email can look like if this is available through your email service provider (MailerLite does do this):

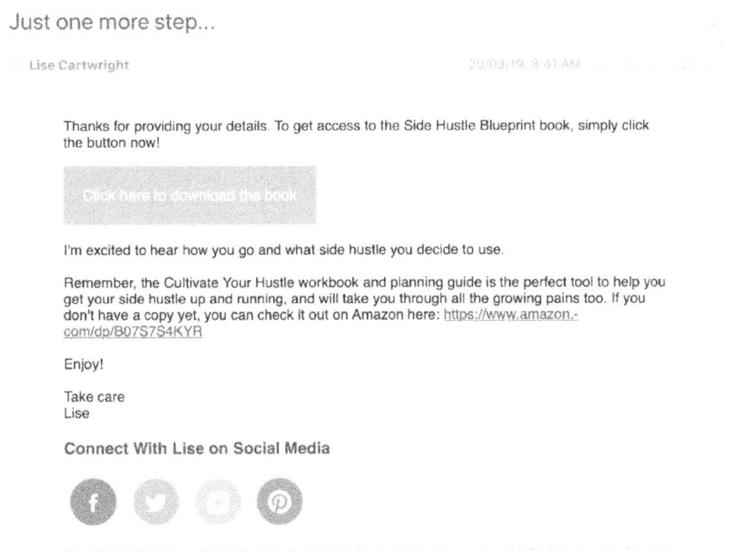
Just one more step...

Lise Cartwright 20/08/19, 8:41 AM

Thanks for providing your details. To get access to the Side Hustle Blueprint book, simply click the button now!

Click here to download the book

I'm excited to hear how you go and what side hustle you decide to use.

Remember, the Cultivate Your Hustle workbook and planning guide is the perfect tool to help you get your side hustle up and running, and will take you through all the growing pains too. If you don't have a copy yet, you can check it out on Amazon here: https://www.amazon.-com/dp/B07S7S4KYR

Enjoy!

Take care
Lise

Connect With Lise on Social Media

You'll find a copy of this email template in the CCC Resource Library here: www.hustleandgroove.com/cccresources.

And that is the end of Part 1: Capture.

YOUR KEY TAKEAWAYS:

1. How to identify your best lead magnet
2. How to capture your ideal leads with opt-in forms and landing pages
3. How to deliver your lead magnets

In the next part, we're going to dive into converting your new leads into customers and what your ideal sales funnel looks like.

And don't freak out! The sales funnel piece is a lot easier than you're thinking… so let's jump straight to it.

Part 2:

CONVERT

"Why waste a sentence saying nothing?"

~ Seth Godin

In this second part of the book, we're going to look at how to convert your new leads into buyers of your amazing products or services.

What makes them stop and say, "Yes! I want this now!" What makes YOU do this with your fav products or services?

As I mentioned previously, everything that I'm sharing with you is neither 'black hat' or icky. It's about providing value first.

You should treat your new leads with the respect and kindness they deserve.

So under no circumstances are you trying to sell them products or services that don't genuinely help them.

Because ain't nobody got time for that!

So what am I talking about here? The first step in conversion is nurturing your awesome leads and then converting them into your best friends and paying customers/clients.

If you get this part of the process right, you'll start to automate your income generation and create a life and business you truly love.

Let's get started!

Step 1:

WELCOME SEQUENCE

Now that you've got your lead magnet, landing pages, and lead magnet delivery email set up, let's make sure your new lead feels welcome!

We want them to stick around for awhile, right?

We want them to be so in love with you and all that you provide, they are literally clamoring to buy your thing.

The best way to make them feel welcome and loved right from the start is to create a great welcome sequence that indoctrinates them into your community.

Now we get to the fun stuff. Setting up your initial welcome sequence for your new email subscribers.

But these aren't just any email subscribers. No. These are your ideal leads. The people you want to work with the most.

So where does the welcome sequence fit in?

Basically, after your lead magnet is delivered, your welcome sequence begins.

You've done the work to get them on your email list, now we need to convert them into the right part of your business that best meets their needs.

The way to do that is to make sure that you start things off on the right foot with a really good welcome sequence.

What is a welcome sequence?

It's a series of automated emails that go out to your new lead based on an event set up in your email platform. Generally, it's triggered to send out 1 day after joining your email list.

It should educate them about you and your business as well as provide them with more value and opportunities to learn more about you and what you provide.

Ideally, your welcome sequence should consist of 5-7 emails, all scheduled to go out one day apart.

Wondering what your email sequence should look like? Let's create one together now.

Let's follow a fictitious business owner, Jane, as she creates her welcome sequence. Her business centers around teaching time management and includes books and a coaching program.

What follows are examples of the emails that would appear after I signed up to Jane's list. The subscriber's name would, ideally, be part of the information you've captured in the opt-in form and can be inserted using code. That way, each email is personalized to the subscriber. Check the help section of your email provider for specifics as well as the resources page link for a quick tutorial.

Day 1 - Email 1: Welcome (plus free gift)

The first email is the welcome email. This is the email that will immediately be sent to anyone who subscribes to your list or opts-in for your lead magnet.

The welcome email is going to do a couple of things.

First, and most importantly, it delivers your free thing.

Since your leads signed up for your list in exchange for something, you absolutely want to be sure they get that something as quickly as possible.

The welcome email will highlight what's to come. The very last thing you want to do is lose people because they thought they were signing up for a free gift and then got a bunch of emails instead.

So be clear and transparent. Tell them you will be sending them a few more emails over the next day or two, and after that they will generally hear from you once or twice a month.

Small things like that will help reduce your unsubscribe rate.

Note: If you've set up your confirmation email to deliver your free gift, this is the email you would send.

Here's a good template you can use to get you started:

Subject: Just one more step…

Hey Lise,

Thanks for providing your details. To get access to the 90-Day Plan simply click the button now!

Click here to download the plan

I'm excited to hear how you go and what your next 90 days look like!

Remember, the Cultivate Your Hustle workbook and planning guide is the perfect tool to help you get your side hustle up and running, and will help you through all the growing pains too. You can apply your 90-day plan to your business easily once you've finished reading the workbook.

If you don't have a copy yet, you can check it out on Amazon here: https://www.amazon.com/dp/B07S7S4KYR

Enjoy!

Take care

Jane

PS: Keep an eye on your inbox for even more value coming your way over the next few days.

Ok, you can see here the welcome email is pretty simple. It delivers the lead magnet, it shows a little bit of your personality and it lays out what the reader can expect from you.

It doesn't have to be too long to get the point across.

Day 2 - Email 2: Did you get it?
This is going to be the first follow-up email. This email is known as the "check-in" email.

You might be surprised to find that even after someone signs up for your free gift and opts into your mailing list, they might not download your lead magnet right away.

It actually happens much more than you think! People are busy and can get distracted, and the last thing you want is for people who might potentially be in love with your products or services (and you) to lose momentum.

So the check-in email serves two purposes.

First, it reminds people about your free gift and second, it gets people used to opening (and receiving) your emails.

This email should be short and to the point, just give them the link to your download and ask them to let you know if they've had any problems.

Here's an example:

Subject: Did you get it?

Hey Lise,

I know you're busy (implementing your 90-day plan I hope!), so I'll keep this short.

I just wanted to check in quickly and make sure you got your free 90-day plan template.

If you didn't, here's that link again:

[insert link here]

If you were able to grab the 90-day plan, I'd love to know what you think of it so far.

Just reply back and tell me your thoughts.

I always love hearing back from my new subscribers and learning more about them and what they'd love to see.

No matter how much or how little you write...

...I read every email.

Talk soon,

Jane

P.S. Don't forget to reply back!

Another simple email. This is just making sure they got the free gift (sometimes people need a little reminder) and asks them to click and reply.

The sooner you can introduce the idea of clicking (either to reply or on a link) to your new subscribers, the better.

You want them to get into that habit. It will come in handy later!

Day 3 - Email 3: Getting Personal

This email is where you want to tell a little bit about your own story.

It will help your new leads feel more of a connection to you. This is especially true if your lead magnet teaches them how to get better at something or fix a problem.

You can relate by showing your own struggles, that you were once in their shoes and now you're not because of these changes.

These types of stories can have a big impact on your audience—when they feel like you are (or were) just like them, the connection is much stronger.

Let's take a look at ant example.

Subject: I'm a recovering procrastinator

Hey Lise,

It wasn't that long ago when I had some of the worst time management of anyone you'd ever met.

Man, was it bad.

I was constantly late for everything...

...doctors appointments, work, my kid's soccer games, I was even late to my own wedding (it's a wonder it even happened at all!).

As you can imagine, my time issues were having a huge (negative) impact on my life. It cost me a big promotion at work, and I was constantly the butt of everyone's jokes.

You know the ones, "Oh tell Jane that dinner is an hour earlier than it really is so she shows up on time."

I'm sure you've heard that one too... and plenty more.

Eventually, I got tired of it.

I was tired of the jokes and feeling rushed all the time, and giving off the impression I was unreliable to my husband, kids, and friends.

That was not a good feeling.

So I decided to make a change.

Wow, it was hard work. I failed a bunch of times. I almost gave up more than a few times, too.

But then I learned this one trick that gave me a huge boost in mastering my time management issues. Now, I talk about it a little bit in my book, [book title] but once I started really embracing this technique, everything changed.

It was the one thing that literally turned everything around...

...I can't wait to share my "secret weapon" to mastering time management with you.

Keep an eye out for the next email and I'll let you in on it. It's going to take your 90-day plan to the next level.

But first, I have a quick favor to ask.

Can you respond back and let me know what your #1 struggle is with time management?

I'd love to see if I can help.

Until then,

Jane

See how this email gets personal?

You can't read it without thinking she really did struggle with time management.

The reason why an email like this works is because it gets personal. Since chances are the subscriber also has time management issues (since they downloaded your lead magnet on creating a 90-day plan), then it's speaking right to their greatest fears.

And, as an added advanced technique, you can use what's called an "open loop" to pique the curiosity of your reader — have them wanting to know more.

This was accomplished by talking about the "secret weapon" to time management.

For the reader who really is struggling with time management and desperately wants a solution, dropping an open-loop like this in the email is going to virtually guarantee they will also read the next email in the series.

This is your aim with the story email.

You need to understand who your target audience is and then speak directly to the things that keep them up at night, because you've felt that way too. And then tell them you have figured out a solution that works.

When you take the time to do that and build a personal relationship, it's laying the foundation for the future... leading them right into your sales funnel for that solution.

Day 4 - Email 4: Tips, Tactics and Hacks

Now remember, in this example our creative business owner is selling books and a coaching program (plus future books) centered around time management.

So you want to have a balance between selling and offering value.

It's always a good idea to offer as much value as you possibly can when it comes to building your email list. You'll never go wrong with that mindset and approach.

So on day 4, you want to give your readers some tips and tactics to help them with their problems.

It's also a good idea to include some of the tactics you use inside your products or services, plus a few tips they haven't heard from you yet.

> *Subject: My #1 time management strategy*
>
> *Hey Lise,*
>
> *I bet you've been waiting anxiously to hear what my big time management "secret discovery" was since our last email.*
>
> *I don't blame you, I was pretty excited to figure this one out myself.*
>
> *After reading about a million books and blog posts on all the tips and tactics I could find, I came up with my own little 5 Point Checklist for Mastering Time Management.*

If you think it sounds simple, that's because it is.

When I first started trying to master time management, I constantly shot myself in the foot by trying to take on too much.

You know how it goes, right?

You want to fix it all so badly, you'll do whatever it takes. And it seems to work, at least for a few days.

Until...

...it's so overwhelming that it actually starts causing more havoc in your life.

Then you're right back where you started.

I did that more times that I want to even admit.

Finally, I started with the tiniest of baby steps.

That helped me build up the confidence to move forward, and became the start of my 5 Point Checklist.

Now I share this plan with all of my coaching clients. In fact it's the very first thing we cover after they get inside the program, that's how much it helps.

As a special bonus gift for you, I'm attaching it here.

[link to 5 Point Checklist]

Hopefully, you will be able to use this "secret weapon" to get started on your own path to being better with time management.

So get reading!

Talk soon,

Jane

P.S. Here's the link again to my 5 Point Checklist [link]. And when you're ready, come check out the Time Management Mastery Workshop, where I cover how to take the 5 Point Checklist and claim back your time to get more done. [link].

This email helps to accomplish a couple of things.

First, it closes the open loop that was set up in the third email, the part about the "secret weapon" to mastering time management.

Second, it does something everyone loves, it gives away something for free! When you give away a "bonus" that's made just for the people on your list, they absolutely love it.

Surprise and delight is what I like to call it. They aren't expecting it, but they love it when they get it. And they love you more.

When you use this tactic, you want to make sure you actually have something of value to give to your new leads. It will really help cement the relationship between the two of you.

Plus, this email helps lead into the idea that you're someone who offers coaching on time management. When you talk about how things work for your clients or students that's a subtle hint that you have been able to help other people get success.

And it tells them you have something to sell. Subtly, but enough that it's not a surprise...

This will lead into the next emails where we get to the concept of pitching.

Let's take a look.

Day 5 - Email 5: Testimonials

Here is where we start to build up a slightly harder push to start selling your products and/or services.

Now, it's easy to do if you've already got a product or service that has helped people. If that's the case, but you don't have any official testimonials yet, there is an easy solution: ask for some.

All you need is one or two testimonials to get the ball rolling.

If your product is brand new and you don't have any client testimonials, then give your product for free to a couple of friends and associates and ask them to use it in exchange for a testimonial.

The same goes for services. Give away one of your service packages to a few people and ask them to give you some honest testimonials on how it has helped them.

Or, use yourself as the testimonial. Explain what life looked liked before and after.

The most important part of having a testimonial is that it provides social proof to potential customers that what you are offering *actually does work.*

Let's take a look:

> *Subject: When you invest in yourself…*
>
> *Hey Lise,*
>
> *One of my absolute favorite clients is Susan.*
>
> *And it's not just because she tells me how awesome I am every time we finish a coaching call :)*
>
> *…though that is nice.*
>
> *No, it's because she's gotten amazing results with her time management. Her progress has blown me away.*
>
> *You see, I bet Susan was a lot like you before she started working with me.*
>
> *She has a good job, a husband she adores, and kids she wishes she could spend more time with. But it always felt like "something" was getting in the way.*

Susan always felt rushed. She was always late to everything (you already know about being the butt of "late" jokes) and ended every single day feeling overwhelmed and frazzled.

Sound familiar?

She was tired of missing out on things with her kids.

Tired of never finding time for a "date night" with her husband.

Tired of getting passed over to lead those important projects at work because she was just too unorganized.

Finally, she'd had enough.

She implemented my 5-Point Checklist, then signed up for my coaching program [link your thing here] and dedicated herself to making a change.

And what a change it's been.

Here's what she has to say:

"Before I worked with Jane, I was one of the most disorganized people you'd ever met. I was always struggling to find more time, I wished there were 25+ hours in the day.

Now, after Jane showed me step by step her time management tools and strategies, I get more done in less time.

I never believed it was possible to actually do it all... and now it is."

See what I mean? Susan went from disorganized mess to supermom just by changing her approach to time management.

That's where I can help.

If you want to find out more from Susan and my other clients who have managed to change their lives, click here [link] to find out more.

Hope to hear from you soon,

Jane

P.S. If you want to really take charge of your time management issues, click here [link] to start today.

So here you should be able to see the power of the testimonial.

What testimonials really do is connect to your readers. It shows that you understand and can help them.

You want to pick a testimonial that speaks directly to your target audience, and their biggest pain point or fears.

They want to see someone who is just like them who has made a change and improved their lives.

If you are able to do that, your path to selling your product or service becomes much easier.

Day 6 - Email 6: Officially Introduce What You Are Selling
Here is where you take the next step in the selling process. In the last email, you gave a testimonial (or two) that teases your product or service. You told them about a person who you helped, a person who likely has very similar problems to the people reading your emails.

This gets them not only interested but helps move them along your sales funnel.

So, here is where you want to see who you can capture to move to the next step and go from a subscriber to a paying client or customer. Leading to consistent income!

Here's an example of how to do it.

Subject: A special invitation for you

Hey Lise,

So in the last email I talked a little about my program. But, I wanted to share a bit more about it here.

Don't worry, I'll keep it short, I know you're busy :)

My program is called 30 Days to Easy Time Management.

In this membership group, we take you from disorganized to super organized in a month. Sound too good to be true?

It's not.

It builds upon my own experience in turning my life around. And, included in the program are over 20 hours of calls and interviews from coaches and time management experts all over the world to help support your journey.

But the best part of the program?

It has to be the online community.

Inside you'll find over 100 other people who are just like you. They've all struggled with time management and have come up with some pretty awesome ways to manage it.

Even I've learned a ton in there!

If you want to check out my 30 Days to Easy Time Management program, here's the link [link], just click it to get started.

If you have any questions about the program at all, don't hesitate to ask.

Talk soon,

Jane

P.S. Oh, I almost forgot to mention!

This is why you should always read the PS :)

Since I really value the people who are on my email list--that's you!--I wanted to offer a special deal.

If you sign up through this email link here [link], in the next 48 hours you get 2 x 30 min 1-on-1 coaching calls with me!.

Sound good?

Can't wait to see you on the inside!

Alright, now your audience knows you officially have a program to offer. And, if you've marketed your lead magnet correctly, you've got a built-in audience ready and waiting for you to show them the solution to their problems.

This is why it's important to choose the right lead magnet. One that is a natural progression into what you sell. It's a big disconnect to your audience if your lead magnet is a makeup tutorial, for example, but your sales funnel leads them into your virtual assistant service!

So back to providing a solution... That's where your product or service is going to come into play. In this email, you give them some information about the program and link to it.

There's no hard sell or anything like that. Some people might be ready to buy immediately, others may be on the fence.

If you want to be a little bit more aggressive, you can do what I did in the PS, offer a bonus that has a time expiration. It can help motivate some of the people who are still deciding and helps your list see that you really do value them because you're giving them a bonus, something they likely *feel* they need to succeed.

Day 7 - Email 7: The Full Sell

Here's where you finally pitch the sale. Since you've been working your way through the list offering your subscribers a lot of value, the pitch won't seem awkward or out of place here. So if you feel awkward at this point, just remember your goal — you want to help people with their problems by offering your product or service. You deserved to be paid for this!

Not to mention, if you've got people following you through six emails in an autoresponder series, you have a pretty good chance of converting them into customers.

Not all, of course, but a much higher percentage than you'd see if you had asked your list to buy something in Email 1, where they don't know you. That's a mistake I see new creatives making. Pitching upfront in their first email... now that is icky...

Here's an example of a *gentle sell email* for a product or service.

> *Hey Lise,*
>
> *What did you think about Susan's story?*
>
> *Pretty inspiring, right?*
>
> *Let me tell you, Susan is not the exception when it comes to my clients. I have helped dozens of people just like her...*
>
> *...just like you.*

Now, if you're still reading, chances are you know you need some help too.

I've given you the 90-day plan system for free, plus a pdf of some of my best tips and strategies on time management.

Some of you might be good to go with just those tools.

Some of you may realize that those free gifts were just the spark in what feels like a very dark tunnel.

But it's a spark that is going to help change your life and take you from disorganized to put-together, almost super-human...

The person you've wanted to be for a long time.

The good news is if you're ready to take that first step, I can help.

The biggest question is, do you want to make the change?

If you do, then now is the time.

Click here [link] to join my coaching program today.

You won't regret it!

Talk soon,

Jane

PS: Let's stay in touch. You don't need to do a thing—you'll get my weekly/bi-monthly/monthly newsletter with time management tips and tricks. If you're not interested, simply click "unsubscribe" below.

And when you're ready, come join the 30-day Time Management Mastery Coaching Program and Membership here [link]

There you have it. Not too pushy, right?

Note: You can grab the swipe file of sample emails on the resources page: www.hustleandgroove.com/cccresources.

By now you have given quite a bit to your list. You've respected their time and space, not spammed them, offered them more free stuff, all of it valuable. Now it's time to ask them to do something for you.

Buy your product or service.

Most people feel squeamish at this part. That's totally normal. But, if you don't ask, it's very hard to get people to buy. Remember that!

So what happens at the end of this welcome sequence?

What happens if someone buys and if they don't?

That's what we're going to cover next!

But first, let's get this set up in MailerLite.

SET UP WELCOME SEQUENCE IN MAILERLITE

It's time to create a campaign in MailerLite, the first step in getting a welcome sequence live.

In MailerLite terminology, a campaign just refers to the emails or newsletters you send out.

From your dashboard click Campaigns. If this is your first campaign, you'll see this message when you go into the Campaigns area.

Click on "create your first email" to get started. You have an option to choose different campaigns based on what you're doing.

Go ahead and choose "regular campaign" which is the first option.

Next you'll need to provide a subject line, confirm who the email is coming from (that's you!) and what language you're sending the email in.

Next, you'll go to the Content portion, which is where you'll choose the Template setup. You've got three options to choose from.

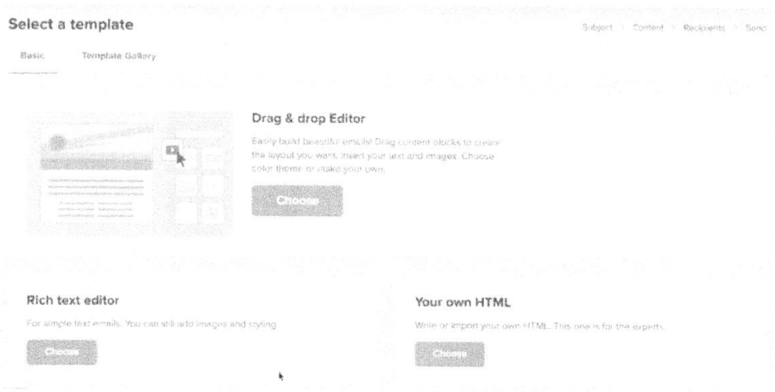

Choose an option that works best for you. I'd recommend the Drag & Drop Editor.

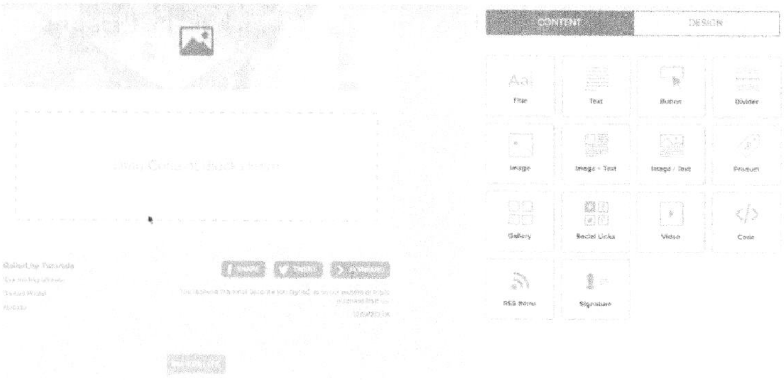

Go through and create your email. You can add images, headings, text blocks. But remember, keep it simple.

When everything looks good, it's time to send. You'll have the option to send now or send in the future. You'll also choose the group that you're sending the email too.

Now you're ready to go!

Every time you want to send out an email series or newsletter, simply repeat the process. This process is similar in other platforms too.

One of the best things about using MailerLite is that it's designed to be very user-friendly. They make everything quite intuitive, and as I've mentioned already, they have a guide to help you along the way as you go through the process.

Now that you've got your welcome sequence set up, let's jump into the main part of this section of the book… converting your ideal leads into customers!

Step 2:

NURTURING YOUR LEADS

This is a crucial step where most business owners end up making a mistake. They take the time to set up an automated welcome sequence and send it out, but then… crickets.

They don't do anything after that. It's a big problem, and I guarantee it will help you lose subscribers (and future customers).

That is the complete opposite of what we're trying to accomplish.

So, when it comes to your email list, even after your welcome sequence is written and loaded, your work isn't done.

In this next section, we'll look at a couple of the most common options that follow the welcome sequence.

Let's get started.

SENDING NEWSLETTERS

One of the more common things to set up after your welcome sequence is finished is a regular newsletter.

A newsletter (also called a broadcast email in some email service providers) is a message that you write and send out at the same time each week or month.

You're probably familiar with these in your own inbox, weekly updates from your local grocery store or monthly updates from your favorite sports team; both are categorized as newsletters.

With a newsletter, you want to strike the right balance. Too many and you'll turn your subscribers off, and too few and they'll forget all about you.

Most creatives should look at sending out newsletters either twice a month or monthly, depending on how much valuable information you can share. This strikes a nice balance.

Of course, it's important to note, if you feel like you don't have anything to say or any news, err on the side of sending your newsletters monthly.

Also, be sure to let your email subscribers know how often you will be sending them regular emails. Consistency is very important here to keep your open rates high and click-through rates even higher.

A newsletter is just a quick overview of what's happening in your life. It provides value to your reader, insight into something they are struggling with. It could be sharing your blog posts, YouTube channel and updates, etc.

Newsletters don't have to be long or drawn out, you can easily take about 10 to 30 minutes to write one and click send. They are a great way to keep in touch with your audience.

You'll find examples of a few of my newsletter emails in the resources page link here: www.hustleandgroove.com/cccresources.

SURVEYS, CONTESTS & GIVEAWAYS

Surveys

If you want to get more people excited about opening your emails, consider the option of running contests and giveaways.

In these, you can get interactive with your list. Not only does it get your subscribers excited to participate, but you can also build up a little bit of goodwill, and maybe even learn some very valuable information.

You'd be very surprised to find the information you can get out of your subscribers--very valuable information--if you simply just ask them.

This is where a survey can come into play. There are a couple of tools you can use, like SurveyMonkey, to create your own survey that's just 3-5 questions and can be emailed out to your entire list.

Ask them what they are struggling with right now. What are they reading? What podcast do they love?

Contests and Giveaways

These are another great option as well. Everyone loves getting something for free, so offer up an Amazon gift card, or your lowest priced offer for free in exchange for helping you by answering questions or spreading the word about you and your business.

NURTURE SEQUENCES

If you want to take things to the next level, then consider setting up automated sequences to handle the following situations:

- New customers
- People who don't buy your thing

These would mean setting up an automated sequence (autoresponder) based on an action your lead takes or doesn't take.

So if someone buys your product or service, what emails would they get next?

You'd at least want to provide them with access to your thing, whether that's via an email with their login details in it or something else.

What else do they need? How will you continue to support them as they work with you or use your product?

And what about the people who don't buy right away? What happens to them?

Sure, you can simply send them your newsletter, that's a good starting point. But what about if you sent them through an autoresponder series that nurtured them further around the solution you're providing.

What if the timing just wasn't right for them? How can you help them while they figure things out?

What type of emails might they need to receive during this period?

Take the time to think through these ideas and then map them out in your email service provider.

By setting these pieces up, you'll go a long way to converting more leads into buyers and then retaining those buyers long-term.

Whew, that was a lot to cover in this part of the book, but you made it!

YOUR KEY TAKEAWAYS:

1. You should know your email service provider inside out
2. Created and implemented a welcome sequence
3. Decided on ways to nurture your leads

In the next part of the book, we're going to focus on captivating those people who bought, but also those who have yet to buy.

Jump in and get started.

PART 3:

CAPTIVATE

"When you treat customers right, they come back… and they tell others."

~ Shep Hyken

In this third part of the book, we're going to look at how to captivate your new leads and customers so that they never want to leave.

Why should you care about captivating them?

Because it's a lot easier to keep a lead or client than it is to go and find new ones… hello? We're not chasing the sale anymore, remember?! If you implement this phase, you'll literally be able to start predicting your income.

As I mentioned previously, everything that I'm sharing with you is neither 'black hat' or icky. It's about providing value always.

You should treat your customers and clients with the respect and kindness they deserve. Like they are your family.

Nurturing them should never stop. So make sure you don't skip over *Part 2: Convert* either, as it all starts with your welcome sequence.

So what am I talking about here? I'm talking about creating amazing experiences for your new leads and for your customers and clients that make them stick around.

If you get this part of the process right, you'll never have to chase the sale again. You'll be able to relax and focus on serving rather than worrying about trying to get new customers or clients.

Consistent income is our goal. It's not our final destination — because it's not all about the money — but it does matter. And if you aren't consistently earning then you're focused on chasing the sale, which sends out negative energy to the Universe and your potential leads. We don't want that.

So the sooner you can consistently create income, the sooner you can focus on growth and positive energy. Life looks very different when you're not worried about when you're getting paid.

Let's get started!

STEP 1:

THE WOW EXPERIENCE

If you really want to captivate your audience, you need to learn how to WOW your customers, clients, and email subscribers.

You need to create an amazing experience so that they never want to leave you.

This is about activating those amazing people that you want to work with or serve into action.

So what does that look like?

First, you need to really understand your target audience. Do you know what they are struggling with, what's keeping them up at night?

Remember back in Part 1: Capture, we talked about surveying your audience? Did you do that?

If you did, you should have the answers to those two questions.

If you didn't, now's the time to do that step.

Do you know what the difference is between a successful creative business owner and one who's just getting by?

The successful creative business owner does whatever it takes to get the answers she needs in order to serve her ideal customer or client. She is constantly checking in with her tribe, seeing how she can best serve them.

The "just getting by" creative business owner, on the other hand, says things like, "Oh, I'll get to that next week. This week, I'm focused on writing 3 new blog posts." She has no idea that her blog posts aren't even being read...

It's time to get a little uncomfortable and do the things that put a catch in your breath.

Step out of your comfort zone.

Your business deserves this information and your target audience deserves your awesomeness.

Don't let a little thing like fear stop you from taking action.

Once you've got an idea of what's keeping your target audience awake at night, think through some of the amazing experiences that you've been through.

So for example, remember when you first joined a membership site, or when you first joined a subscription? Has there been any business that stood out in terms of what they were doing and made you feel amazing?

Some awesome experiences I've had recently include:

ConvertKit

When I joined ConvertKit. After setting up my account and completing all the steps, they sent me an email congratulating me on this success.

Then they said that because I'd done everything they asked, I could get a t-shirt and care package at their cost. Who doesn't want that?!

ConvertKit continues to be amazing in the way that they serve. Their customer service is one of the best I've ever had access to. They are constantly helpful and always quick to respond to help requests.

I have been with ConvertKit for close to 4 years now and I have no desire to move anytime soon!

Niche Spa

This is a local bricks & mortar business that my husband and I go to frequently to get hot stone massages and relaxing facials.

After our first visit, aside from the outstanding service provided during our visit, they followed up with an email to check in on how we were feeling and to offer us a 15% discount on our next booking.

They have also sent me a voucher on my birthday for $100 discount on any service, which is extremely generous.

They have this gorgeous waiting room that has big, comfy couches, luxurious pillows and lots of yummy treats to tuck into while you wait.

We love going there because it's so relaxing... exactly what we want!

Kajabi

Another great experience upon joining. Kajabi goes the extra mile and assigns you an account manager. This account manager jumps on a call with you and makes sure you're all set up. And not just a quick 15-minute call, although that is also available for one-off help. No, this is a 45-minute call where they get to know you and help you in your business.

Kajabi is where my membership site, Hustle HQ, is located.

They sent me a ton of training videos and emails once I joined and continue to check in on my progress.

They also celebrate milestones with you! As soon as I reached the $1,000 mark in revenue, they sent me a care package with a t-shirt, stickers etc.

It shows how much they care about your success and I love this.

Hopefully this gives you some ideas as to why creating a WOW experience for your customers or clients is important.

Wowing your audience is how you will differentiate your business from somebody else in the same niche who's providing exactly the same product or service as you.

It's your time to shine!

WOW EXPERIENCE IDEAS

Struggling to come up with what might be a great way to WOW your audience?

Here are some ideas that you can get started with:

#1: Sending your brand new client or customer a thank you card in the physical mail.
I'm talking snail mail here. Now this means that you need to have their postal address. And if you're selling digital products or services, you aren't necessarily capturing that information.

But there is a way around that. There is a service called Postable.com that allows you to capture these details, plus more.

This service allows you to send out cards via snail mail to your customers and clients. You'll get notified when it's their birthday, when it's their wedding anniversary, and anything else you ask about and they provide the answer to.

In some locations, they also include gift cards as well.

This is definitely an easy service to set up and WOW your new lead/customer/client right from day one.

#2: Send a coffee gift card.
You could also send out a coffee gift card after your new member has been in your membership for 14 days.

You can use something like Starbucks, or find out their local brew… there's loads of online options for doing this. You just gotta think outside the box.

#3: Send digital gift cards.

You could also send them a $5 Amazon gift card, or any other digital gift card. E-cards are amazing and easy to get into the hands of your ideal customer or client.

But we're looking to WOW our audience, so if you can send something physical in the mail, it will make you stand out. Your new customer or client will not be expecting this from you.

And when they do receive it, they will feel amazing and fall in love with you and your creative business.

So that takes care of when they become a new client or customer.

But what about after their first 30 days?

EXTENDING THE WOW EXPERIENCE

The goal is to set up a system that allows you to consistently WOW your clients and customers.

After the first 30 days, if you've done some of the options above, you will have cemented the relationship.

But you need to make this continue.

So what can you do?

Figure out the best milestones for continuing to WOW them.

How long does your service go for? Your goal is to map out a timeline of WOW experiences during this time.

Let's take a membership site, for example. Let's say the membership lasts for 12 months.

In the first 30 days, you'd send a card and Amazon e-gift card to a new member.

At the 90-day mark, you send them a coffee card and your fav sweet treat to congratulate them on their progress.

At the 6-month mark, you decide to shine a light on them via social media, telling everyone online how amazing they are.

At the 9-month mark, you gift them a 30-minute 1-on-1 coaching call with you to discuss their next steps and help get them unstuck.

And at the 12-month mark, you enrol them for another 12 months inside your membership and give them a 5% discount for sticking with it. You also send them a card with a little something special included.

To recap, it would look like this:

- First 30 days, send a Postable card and e-gift card
- 90-days, send coffee card
- 6-months, shout on social media
- 12-months, re-enrol with a 5% discount

This is an awesome WOW experience and your customer or client is going to never want to leave.

You're going to surprise and delight them as often as you can.

It really is the little things that count.

So think about things that might make sense to do that are easy to implement and that don't cost you a ton of money.

And if you're selling a high end product or offer, like anything over $1,000 dollars for example, then it's worth it to send them some type of gift basket once they join, don't you agree?

Etsy is awesome for this type of thing. You can jump on Etsy, get something custom made for that client and shipped straight to them.

Remember, it's about creating an amazing, WOW experience from your ideal customer or clients perspective… not about what's the most beneficial to you.

Now that you've decided what your WOW experience is going to look like, let's figure out how to automate this as much as possible.

STEP 2:

SET IT ON AUTOPILOT

Before we jump into automating the WOW experience, it's important that you differentiate what you'll do for new leads versus what you'll do for your customers or clients.

In the previous step, we really focused on the customer/client experience, but you should apply something similar to your new leads, those that join your email list.

Particularly if you're looking to continue to attract your ideal clients to you.

We all know that your ideal leads have already received a digital gift of some description… so how can you extend the WOW experience to them without spending a ton of money on postage?

Here are some ideas:

1. Gift them a copy of your lowest paid product (ideally something that costs under $47) if they open your emails and engage with you within the first 30 days
2. Send them an e-gift card at the 90-day mark if they have opened 80% of your emails in the past 90 days
3. Gift them a complimentary 15-minute hot seat call with you at the 6-month mark

4. Shout them out on social media if you see them promoting your stuff (do this anytime)

Remember, it's the little things that count!

AUTOMATE YOUR WOW EXPERIENCE

Take the time to map out what your WOW experience looks like for each of your 'buckets' aka leads, clients, products etc.

Then decide on the milestones or frequency with which each action will take place.

For example, if you're working with a one-on-one coaching client, you might have a task to send them a Postable.com card within 7 days of them signing up.

Then, you might have gifts assigned to go out at 90-days, 6 months and 12 months. Map that out in your calendar or fav to-do app.

Then, as you sign up a new coaching client or customer, you can go and add the tasks to your calendar or to-do app so that you get reminded of when to take action.

Do this for your leads as well. Except this process might be more of a review process for each milestone or frequency, where you check these monthly and take action accordingly.

Implement this phase and you'll really stand out to your ideal customers and clients and it's also how you'll attract the right leads and keep them on your list.

And it works. I've had a number of different customers or existing clients reach out to me who say, "Hey Lise, I knew it was right to work with you because you just sent me this amazing card…" It's just that little thing that doesn't really cost you much but shows that you care.

Your task is to come up with some different ideas that might be a good fit for your creative business.

Choose what those milestones or frequency pieces are and then implement!

Create your milestone map and to-do items. Automate them using services like Dubsado.com or 17hats.com.

The point is to take action now. Set it up in your Google Calendar to get started if something like Dubsado isn't right for you now.

Don't use technology as an excuse to not do this step!

YOUR KEY TAKEAWAYS:

1. You should have a list of WOW experience ideas ready to implement
2. A map of milestones for creating WOW opportunities for your new customers and leads
3. An automated process so that you don't forget to do any of these things!

And that's it. You've just finished *Part 3: Captivate.*

This was the final piece in the Capture, Convert, Captivate method.

If you truly want a creative business that excites you, that fills your soul, and serves the audience you care about, this method will help you achieve that.

It will also help you start to map out what consistent income might look like for your business.

But reading this book isn't enough. You need to take action.

In the next chapter, you'll learn how to take everything you've just learned and turn it into strategic action.

You got this. I believe in you. Your ideal customers and clients believe in you too.

Ready? Let's jump straight in to your 30-Day Action Plan.

CAPTURE, CONVERT, CAPTIVATE 30-DAY ACTION PLAN

One of the biggest obstacles for most creative business owners in implementing these three components is that they don't have the right strategy or focus to begin with.

They don't know what to expect or where to start.

So instead of moving forward, they file it away for a later date.

That's why I want to provide you with a clear action plan on what to do next.

How to take what you've just learned and put it into practice.

We'll start by dividing a 30-day time frame into three 10-day phases.

Each phase will focus on capturing, converting, and captivating your ideal audience.

It'll help you remove the roadblocks so you can stick to a plan and put it into place.

It will also allow you to identify where your gaps are and get started on filling those in.

But most of it all, it will allow you to create a plan for establishing real relationships with your ideal audience.

Building the know/like//trust factor so that you can transition into predictable income-generating months.

DAYS 1-10: PHASE ONE - CAPTURE

Over the next 10 days, you're going to focus on the pieces that will capture the attention of your ideal target audience... the people you really want to work with.

You'll figure out what your best lead magnet is, create it and set it up, ready to be delivered to your new leads.

DAYS 11-20: PHASE TWO - CONVERT

In this next 10-day phase, you'll focus on setting up your email service provider, creating autoresponders that convert your new leads into willing and long-term subscribers and ultimately, customers or clients.

DAYS 21-30: PHASE THREE - CAPTIVATE

In the last 10-days, you'll focus on creating the most amazing WOW experience for your leads, clients or customers. You'll spend time mapping out the milestones and setting up all the pieces to automate this process.

Get access to the 30-day action plan at
www.hustleandgroove.com/cccplan.

A Final Note to the Reader

As we near the end of this book, I wanted to take a moment to tell you that you don't have to be perfect about this stuff.

The whole point in capturing, converting, and captivating your ideal audience is to connect with your people.

To continue to develop relationships.

To make an impact and change the lives of those you touch.

And this means letting go of things needing to be perfect or 'just right' before you implement them.

You might not think it's worthwhile creating a lead magnet. But if you want to attract the right leads, how do you plan on doing that?

Sending out regular emails might not be your thing, but how can you expect your ideal customer or client to know what you provide if you're not telling them about it?

Your job, as a creative business owner, is to create the things you're passionate about.

But if you want to be a profitable creative, it means that you also have to step back and put your business hat on every so often.

By putting the right systems in place and automating as much of this process as possible, you can focus on creating while also working smarter and letting the tools available to you to do the heavy lifting.

At the end of the day, you know your business best. Do what makes the most sense to you.

But don't do nothing.

I'm certain that if you take action, implement the 30-day action plan, and follow through on what you set out to do, you will become a lead attracting machine... but not attracting just any lead.

You'll be attracting the right lead.

Remember, it's far easier to make money from your existing leads, clients or customers, than it is to find new leads.

Focus on engaging, encouraging, and captivating the people you are already serving and your creative business will start to take on a very different feel.

I believe you can do this.

And if you're stuck, just take a deep breath and ask yourself this question: "What's my immediate next step?" And do that step.

Ready to create an online business that amplifies your you-nique gifts, strengths, and talents? Grab your FREE business personality profile chart here: https://www.hustleandgroove.com/bizprofile

I can't wait to hear about your success!

Send me your thoughts and suggestions.
Lise@hustleandgroove.com.

Take care

Lise

About the Author

Lise is a full-time author and coach. She is a self-confessed shoe fanatic – like obsessed. Just ask her husband!

She has been looking for the magic in life since she was first exposed to positive, happy thoughts at the tender age of one — thanks Mum and Dad!

Lise can regularly be found at local cafes, NOT drinking coffee, but the more sophisticated and magical beverage that is a Chai Latte.

Lise helps budding creatives to inspire and connect with their tribe through mindset optimization, online marketing, and productivity strategies.

You can find out more about how Lise can help you more via her website: www.hustleandgroove.com.

Want to see more of the books Lise has written? You can find them here: www.hustleandgroove.com/booksbylise.

Can You Help?

If you enjoyed this book, could you PLEASE leave an honest review from where you purchased your copy from?

Reviews are really important to the success of a book — so if you like (or don't like!) what you've read, PLEASE take 2 minutes to leave your honest review — I really appreciate it.

Made in the USA
Monee, IL
26 January 2026

42454063R00066